TRUE, FALSE, NONE OF THE ABOVE

The Poiema Poetry Series

Poems are windows into worlds; windows into beauty, goodness, and truth; windows into understandings that won't twist themselves into tidy dogmatic statements; windows into experiences. We can do more than merely peer into such windows; with a little effort we can fling open the casements, and leap over the sills into the heart of these worlds. We are also led into familiar places of hurt, confusion, and disappointment, but we arrive in the poet's company. Poetry is a partnership between poet and reader, seeking together to gain something of value—to get at something important.

Ephesians 2:10 says, "We are God's workmanship . . ." *poiema* in Greek— the thing that has been made, the masterpiece, the poem. The Poiema Poetry Series presents the work of gifted poets who take Christian faith seriously, and demonstrate in whose image we have been made through their creativity and craftsmanship.

These poets are recent participants in the ancient tradition of David, Asaph, Isaiah, and John the Revelator. The thread can be followed through the centuries—through the diverse poetic visions of Dante, Bernard of Clairvaux, Donne, Herbert, Milton, Hopkins, Eliot, R. S. Thomas, and Denise Levertov—down to the poet whose work is in your hand. With the selection of this volume you are entering this enduring tradition, and as a reader contributing to it.

—D.S. Martin
Series Editor

True, False,
None of the Above

MARJORIE MADDOX

CASCADE *Books* · Eugene, Oregon

TRUE, FALSE, NONE OF THE ABOVE

Cascade Books
An Imprint of Wipf and Stock Publishers
199 W. 8th Ave., Suite 3
Eugene, OR 97401

PAPERBACK ISBN 13: 978-1-4982-3922-6
HARDCOVER ISBN 13: 978-1-4982-3924-0

Cataloguing-in-Publication data:

Maddox, Marjorie.

True, false, none of the above / Marjorie Maddox.

xvi + 92 pp. ; 23 cm.

The Poemia Poetry Series

ISBN: 978-1-4982-3922-6 (paperback) | ISBN: 978-1-4982-3924-0 (hardback)

1. American Poetry—21st Century. I. Title. II. Series.

PS3725 M28 2016

Manufactured in the USA.   03/23/2016

For all my teachers and students.

And for my husband, Gary:

fellow reader, writer, and teacher.

It was that first conversation on faith and literature

that began our story.

"The type of mind that can understand good fiction. . . is at all times the kind of mind that is willing to have its sense of mystery deepened by contact with reality, and its sense of reality deepened by contact with mystery."

−MYSTERY AND MANNERS: OCCASIONAL PROSE,
FLANNERY O'CONNOR

Contents

Preface

True, False, None of the Above poetically explores what it means to write, read, and teach literature in a world that—at turns—rejects, embraces, or shrugs indifferently at the spiritual.

This is a book on the intersection of words and belief, on what it means to be a poet of faith, on how books mark and mirror our lives, and how sometimes the journey we experience on the page leads us to faith.

As a Christian and as a professor of English, I believe literature has very much to do with our lives. It is not an escape from, but rather a confrontation with reality, a reality that includes the overarching struggles of the soul. Flannery O'Connor once said, "I write to discover what I know." Joan Didion echoed, "I write entirely to find out what I'm thinking, what I'm looking at, what I see and what it means. What I want and what I fear." *True, False, None of the Above* examines how writing, reading, and teaching lead us to discovery by bringing us face-to-face with the world we live in and the world to come.

On Defining Education

*"Training is everything. The peach was once a bitter almond;
cauliflower is nothing but cabbage with a college education."*

–Mark Twain

Isn't the seed better,
its tough, hard case
beneath the juice?
Flesh? Just so much puffing up,
skin gone soft with too much rouge.
Better to be tossed out than consumed,
lusted after by the colon.

Or what of that lower-class cabbage
shredded to bits, thrown haphazardly in soups?
Whole, she's the Cinderella that steals the show
for the truly hungry.

Nobody likes cauliflower
cowering on fine china,
the ugly sister decorated
with a sterling ladle's worth of cheese.

Please, feel free to confront.
I'm not talking about who you should be
but are. Let's start with the essence of seed
and see what sprouts from there.

How Spiritual Are You?

-Time *magazine quiz, 10/25/04*

Tallying twenty *True* or *False*
answers to wishy-washy visions, I'm translated
from a poet of faith into
    "a practical empiricist lacking self transcendence"
according to a noted psychologist
touted as today's expert.
I don't like flunking and try again.
Any room for fudging? To insert faith? Even a seed of the spiritual?
    "extrasensory perception"?
    "completely unaware of things going on around me"?
    "I love the blooming of flowers . . . as much as seeing an old friend"?
Though I scan and re-scan, all I can check with confidence
is the final slot—the quizmaster's definition of extreme?—
    "I believe miracles happen."
A half-dozen more statements I rationalize as "sometimes,"
insulted by society's synonyms of "spiritual" and "spacey."
As a poet, I should be used to this
but gain no points from that either.
A sidebar promises to explain a "God gene"
inherent in some of us—a cultural twist on predestination
that leaves me unable to select the first square:
    "I often feel so connected to the people around me
    that it is like there is no separation between us."
Where is the "stranger in a strange land" line?
Where is the question, "Do you believe
in one God, the Father Almighty. . .?"

Euchre and Eucharist

"I like to play euchre.
He likes to play Eucharist."

—Robert Frost on T. S. Eliot

Something there is that doesn't love a game,
that wants its end. The telephone, the other
world clanging to get in.

And yet the end
is where we start from. And every trick
that is right (where every play is at home,
taking its place to support the others)
brings us to the dealing.

Pass the wine.

Trump is the still point of this shuffled world,
miracles and tricks hidden by the other.

Good neighbors make good partners.
This is my hand. Take, eat.

This is my ace, which was dealt for you;
bet in remembrance of me.

In this garden of numbers
that promise redemption,
picking apples is a distraction.
Focus on five sacraments of points;
pray unceasingly.

Each suit, a pattern of timeless moments,
speaks its own liturgy, wants the red-and-black
of blood-and-sin.

Hope is the cruelest game, breeding
lies out of the dead hand, mixing
memory and desire.

Here is the man with three staves, and here the Wheel,
and here is the one-eyed merchant, and this card,
which is blank, is something he carries on his back,
which I am forbidden to see.

We pick what we cannot know,
believe what we cannot see,
try to get away from earth awhile
and then come back to it and begin over.

O to be a swinger of chalices!
To consume the earthly incense of cigarettes,
the confessions of cards.

We die with the dying:
See, they depart, and we go with them.
We are born with the dead,
plastic chips on our tongues.

There are hours to go before I sleep.
I play much of the night and go south in the winter.

Invention

I'm tired of plugged-in words
while rain drips across its own screen of sky.
And yet, earlier, a lightning bug flitted across my mind,
a blip of summer's paradox—
rest and productivity—this
"official state insect," fly of fire-inspiring epiphany,
doomed diplomat of the hole-punched jar
that almost perched upon these letters
but recognized death early enough to flee
to untyped pastures

and wound up in Philadelphia's past
in Franklin's head,
trying to buzz lightbulb-bright possibilities
across the dark screen of invention,
the fear of ridicule jeering
from the corner of his mind
as that jolt of fireflies
zigzagged like a kite
across night's horizon,
looking for voltage and rain.

Radical

*"I never dared be radical when young
for fear it would make me conservative
when old."*

–Robert Frost

This is the place to rebel:
the top of arching treetops,
sky raunchy in red,
the wind kicking up a ruckus.
Nature is never tame or unforgiving,
the least safe escape from ourselves
because it echoes back in each twig creak
the bones we hobble on
looking for a mountainous Babel
that lets us come and go
from here to the ethereal
and back. Tell folks you write
landscapes, and they'll nod,
buy a book for a cousin in Vermont
without any suspicion of violence
bushwhacking through the words
thick as the local vernacular.
No sweet violets here
polka-dotting the lawn.
A tree is a tree is a tree is a birch
and night a close acquaintance,
shivering from the frost.

And the Topic for Today is Environmentalism. . . .

Teaching "God's Grandeur"

More politically correct than divine grandeur,
it too flames out in this small Pennsylvania town
where fracking hijacks the headlines. Good reason
and good enough to bring the state students trodding
heavily into a poem piled high with God and earth,
with "responsibilities" they hear each morning
as the gas industry trucks rattle past our windows,
their tired drivers knowing nothing
of iambic pentameter or sestets but much
about food on the table, a steady job.

The freshmen, eager now,
blurt out *dilemma, paradox, instress*—
and all those other new-sounding ideas
suddenly connected to their lives,
their parents, the sonnet
they think was written last week,
even with its 19th century,
sound-packed syllables they don't get
until slowing down, thinking.

And so—after playing with light, foil, sound;
the way trade "sears," "blears," and "smears";
and how and why shoes separate us from ground—
we detour to Genesis, Cat Stevens, and a heavy metal rendition
that almost drowns out Hopkins with bass.
All this before rounding the terrain-raked bend
to solution, which is what—they are surprised to discover—
we all most want: the eloquent octet, the bright wings,
the *ah!* that opens the mind to talk,
at long last, about the holy.

Louise

for Louise Erdrich

Again, the space
between words lures you
into the clearing between
German and Chipewyan,
a butcher's knife or tomahawk
poised at each stanza,
lines slashed open
like the split deer
transformed to spirit
still thrashing about
inside you.

Arisen, you stretch,
arch your back—
lovely, sleek, survivor.
Your many young follow,
timid, graceful,
their bright night eyes
beautifully interpreting
the light
in the wounded world.

Teaching Frost

Fresh from Pittsburgh or Philly,
they relax in the familiar quote,
raise hands willingly,
plagiarize a "bad-ass" teacher
from summer school
the year before last
who saw in them the rough stones
of a road traveled
less than I-79 or the Northeast Extension
to here, small-town PA,
where I'll un-teach all
those *this = that* interpretations,
and we'll rev up the engines again,
pull out in a new direction,
complicated with tiered highways
and misdrawn maps.

But first, their faces
rocky with knowledge,
with *this-poem-stuff-ain't-so-bad*,
even that semi-secret *sometimes-I-write-poetry* glint
while looking at the book, at me, at their bro reading,
looking anywhere but out the window
back to those *I-don't-give-a-damn* days,
telling me it's all going to be OK,
and we can start,
and we can go
wherever the poem takes us.

History

is what we keep rereading into months,
decades, the unremembered squares of years
fenced between us, crabgrass, brown-edged lilacs;

is what we memorize like dog-eared almanacs,
or blandly hopeful seed packs
flattened in bottom drawers;

is what—across rusting shelves in backyard sheds—
become our snippets of care and compost,
stacked rectangles of warning. And yet,

we make good neighbors, two yards of well-
mowed yearning, tamed gardeners still coveting
each other's most unruly seasons.

Parable

"Virtue! a fig! 'tis in ourselves that we are thus or thus.
Our bodies are our gardens, to the which our wills are gardeners."

—Othello, William Shakespeare

"Virtue! A fig!" We grasp the hoe and dig.
The dirt we turn is taken from ourselves.
We chop the trunk and bough; then clip the twig,
and this way prune the molecule and cell.
The slender stalk, the brown and drooping blooms
obey the will within our working hands.
But evening falls and weariness consumes.
Both self and garden disobey commands.
O faithless workers, wake! The Gardener prays
while you sleep sound as seeds inside this wall.
The weeds take root; the best earth turns to clay.
What dirt-clad Adam sowed becomes *our* Fall.
We're the compost, fools; we're "the fig."
The time is short. Come grasp the hoe and dig.

The Joke Around the Water Cooler
and Other Dilemmas

Let us nail ourselves to him and resist
temptation's lure to mock the one
who loves us most. Surely this
is the serpent's curse: angel outdone

by temptation's lure. We mock: one
sinister hiss and pride slithers in.
As serpents, we curse angels, done
with the debt we owe. Sin's

sinister hiss: a pride that slithers in
to our reason till we forget
the debt we owe. Ah, sin's
glide into the lives we've kept

shiny with reason till we forget
the garden serpent still hisses
and glides into our lives. We've kept
its skin near even as we miss his

garden. "Come back," the thirsty snake hisses,
"I love you most. Surely this
skin is like his. The world's here. Don't miss it
for nails and him. He wants you for himself. Resist."

Lower Higher Ed

Here *God*
gums up in the mouth,
won't spit itself out
with every easy expletive,
leaving the discussion free
for disagreement.

Harder
to digest than politically correct
sex, shit, or *Shades of Grey,*
it then tries to slide
down the coarse slope
of the throat,
but won't.

Or rather
can't, catching instead
on the inside of each
tongue-in-cheek,
a wedge of weighty
popular propositions.

Show-stopper,
thought-lasher, can't-believe-you-
believe quasher, eyes as wide as
some size-ten foot in a mouth
trying to chew through
the ultimate classroom

taboo
while you wonder why
the syllable turns
rancid, *whosoever shall*

deny me fanatically churning
bile in a belly of half-
digested
               Truth.

The Fourth Man

His face is the greater flame
but doesn't flicker. No furnace
fuels his glory. "Son of gods,"
the king calls out and cowers from the heat.
Sparks crown our heads.
We are un-singed and sing of seraphs,
genuflect before his servant,
ten times as golden as any man-made
Hades that can't consume
the luminous, the purified,
the once-upon-a-time burning bush,
the evermore-ignited blaze
of Yahweh.

Distinctions

*"There is one notable dead tree . . .
the inscape markedly holding its
most simple and beautiful oneness. . . ."*

                                   –Gerard Manley Hopkins' journals

Inscape

Curled into this moment,
swirled into this tree,
epiphany with a capitol *E*,
an ordained extraordinary gene
translated to mean uniquely
breathed into being and why
the world sings its key
of awe.

Instress

Such power to hold the whole
symphonic cosmos, spring pushing up
into twig and Trinity, each leaf
cradled by Creator, the Spirit
breathing its force field
of sentience, circling the sense
of our being that now—
this moment or the next—
breaks open its seed
of seeing.

Lucille

for Lucille Clifton

Your name breaks out
as light in the eyes
of the poems
radiating from your lips,
enlightening so jovially
about pain that the beams
strike hard
at the near-sightedness
we perch on our
non-olfactory noses
in the dim theater
where you read
about light
in the bright darkness
that surrounds us.

Globe

not of the world
but of glass,
an upside-down bonnet
for those light bulbs
whose heels dig in
to the ceiling

not of the earth
but our world,
almost shards of loss
when the bolts
loosened,
the faux-crystal shattering
inches from the eyes
of our daughter,
who was reading

not of the world
but of that world
beyond this breakable globe
of earth, so fragile
in its breaking of words,
in its broken need for mercy.

Hulga

"Then she had gone
and had the beautiful name,
Joy, changed. . . ."

–"Good Country People,"
Flannery O'Connor

And when you turn your multi-pierced nose,
your purple hair, and your Sistine-chapel neck
this way, do you hear her clichés
tumbling from my Good Country mouth?
Spite is the lip ring you tongue
when joy thumps like a limb hollowed out
of hope. Our Good Book is full
of empty and both of us
are conned. But wait,
there's more tale
at the end
of this leg
of the
story.

Orpheus: the Fugitive Kind

for Tennessee Williams

I. Descending

Birds the color of sky flap their notes of freedom,
accompany your only companion of string-sung love
that serenades all the female living. Snakeskin,
listen to your own soul: all that is wild howls for release
and still you descend degree by degree
to thaw the frozen lady married to Hades' home
fires. The path is cold and winding. How long
can machismo strum its fiery truth,
can the music of your muscles
lift up the bitten in its Blues?

2. Ascending

All answers come in the seduction of loneliness,
the turn of the neck, the twist of the body,
the sweet lure to save what's fallen
behind, or—like Eurydice, like Lot's wife, like Lady—
the consummating desire to see
once more a charred orchard that smolders
between the notes almost above
the Underworld, where, yes,
even the blue jays now sing
a southern dirge for the fugitive
and the fetus.

Father's Day

*"In Mill Hall, a man kills his sons
and himself. . . ."*

−newspaper headline

He unwrapped the Timex,
snapped it on his wrist,
and shot three sons flat in a mobile home.

Like any story you read,
it becomes you turning
the gun on yourself.
It becomes you, watching.

The slim house. One thought
stirring the others. They whir,
churn with the washer's dirt,
bleed colors into pattern.

All map is pattern, connecting
thought, home, town; disconnecting
into arrows clipped to the hitch of a house.

If he killed his sons for revenge: "Cold-blooded."
If he added himself: "Crazy!"
It clicks like that, wheels into the mind
spinning out of town, any road
with stones large enough to throw.

Those Isaacs lift gifts,
motion in their eyes.

At night, newsprint blurs
inside the swirls of your iris.
Headlines hide behind lids.

Still you read
histories of yourself
in others, those gone wrong
or right, all directions relative
to where you are. You drive
to keep from sleeping, accelerate quickly
over crossroads, "the closest,"
your own father says, "those suicides
get to the bloody cross."

The Storm Before the Calm

*"The tempest in my mind
Doth from my senses take all feeling else
Save what beats there."*

—*King Lear*, William Shakespeare

She doesn't know what rages, but each night
the pain, unpinned from logic, begins its slow spin
toward howl. Her words, flung in the vortex,
circle accusations, fly out at us
stunned into silence while the tempest
in her brain keeps howling. Each night
she doesn't know what rages. We circle
her flailing body, try to unpin her pain
from the vortex that spins her howl.
Logic keeps silent. Night flies out at us,
accusing. It is a slow spin, this rage
that unpins her, flings her into a vortex
she cannot name. Her brain's tempest
is the howl circling our nights. We flail
in silence, circling rage. Night unpins
our bodies. She doesn't know.
The tempest in her brain keeps howling
until rage unpins its pain
from vortex and out
flies silence.

Watch vs. Warning

"Female-named hurricanes kill more
than male hurricanes because people
don't respect them, study finds."

—Washington Post, 6/2/14

Surely the whirling of this world
into some wind-gone-wild transport
to Oz-opposite names all tree-thrashing terrors
or should, a double-edged Saffir-Simpson scale
of nurture/nature of respect in respect to
whose wrath shakes our quaking spirit
more, which also is just breath gone haywire,
this life built in the lungs and expired
into air as turbulent as any cascading
into climate-crashing crescendo
off the coast of somewhere.
Dorothy/Don, this isn't
Kansas anymore.
Each day,
the breeze
and we
pick up
more
vio-
lent-
ly
brok-
en.

Swept Away

Texas Homecoming Queen Swept Away

                              –*USA Today* headline, May 26, 2015

The usual warnings—"Drive
carefully," "Don't
drink," "Don't get swept away
with passion," "Come home
safe, whole, pure, early,
now"—all words
we've heard, as we pinned on
that corsage; all prayers we've mouthed
as our child sailed out the door
on the arm of a tuxedoed or sequined date
toward the American rite of passage.

That was before the rain started. Before
floods crashed the after
party. Before Texas and Oklahoma,
and even before, in my own hometown,
two teens swerved into danger,
into death, on the windy path home
from prom, celebration of indestructibility.

Alyssa, ignore all
our adult pleas for respectability. Listen
instead to the storm crying
its warning, to the wind
winding up its crescendo
of destruction. Stop dancing
and leave with the wrong crowd, or break
curfew, dance longer,
and stay, the quick beat of the rain
your rhythm of living,
twirling you on and on

into a day dawning only
with the small, innocuous storms
of parental worry.

No Shadow of Turning

"with whom is no variableness. . . ."
—James 1:17

Everything tilts and turns,
this smog-filled sphere spinning
lopsidedly in the space

we too casually abandon to chaos.
We cluster constellations into stories
we want to tell children

hungry for heroes
and earthbound gods
unsure of their footing

but leave the creeds hovering
in some other galaxy
we've forgotten to breathe in.

Such momentum of disbelief!
Such dizzying struggle
to pivot with all perspectives!

Stop. Be still and know.
The Trinity's still point
throws no shadow.

Corresponding Reporter

Again, thunder without rain,
so much commotion clap-clapping dry air,
and me, a trillion miles away circling some other planet,
looking down, humming a dance of downpour
on my heart or even a sprinkle of spring shower
on the left pinkie of my soul, the ghost-of-a-chance still
down there in the arid before the afterlife I'm floating toward;
hard to tell when meteors join the mix, and tiny five-pointed stars—
as shiny as the one on my childhood nativity
with the cracked Wisemen and smiling Mary—
fly toward my eyes like knats I need to swat away
before lightning does, after all, saw through space—
a jagged breadknife of sharp—and all this clutter
of image and orbiting metaphors melts in the final burn
of descent, then—can it even be—condenses
to a single drop of wet I can taste
in a throat parched
but open, waiting
to drink.

Prayer

"a flight of the heart towards
the throne of God."

–St. Joseph Cafasso

How the air
of prayer

breathes and buoys—
not words,

not even the slight lift
of almost-thought, but less/

more; who can tell
the teaspoon of light

beneath wings that tilt,
just so, toward eternity?

It is the breeze
of eyelids closing,

the wind
of knees bending,

the mind
without knowing

soaring beyond
what we know of beyond.

The Prophecy of Birds

The Raven

knew flight over waters when all there was
was wet, the ark lost behind the smooth arch
of wings, only a thin line of air
between green sea and grey sky,
then forever and forever
washed up with the slap
of wave against wave.
What weariness to circle
the same expanse,
the echo of rain,
even the wind
unable to land,
looking,
looking.

The Dove,

pale
shadow
tracing the raven's
soar above an earth-
turned-sea, seeking—
for seven days—any inch
of dry, finding only the man's
chapped hand. The second week,
its flight fingered the tops of waves
that fingered the tops of trees, releasing,
finally, twigs of green ready for the dove's sleek beak.
Its last journey knew no U-turns, just a straight flight
to elsewhere, brimming with bushes, drenched orchards
hungry for song, *hallelujahs* hanging from every waiting bough.

Same Song, Different Kid

−Psalm 96.1

For each unwashed,
     egg-crusted,
          disgusting dish of yuck;
   for unmatched, foot-high piles
            of socks; for the overflowing
    day-old Glad bag
       of chicken bones smack inside
          the door he just went out;
for all teen and toddler temper tantrums, so like
    my own,
         Father: outbursts of doubts,
  daily distractions,
        new fads of faith;
           weekly whines,
the done and undone.
    O slow-to-anger, quick-to-love,
Papa, hear my plea to be
         a new song.

Laundry List

*"The ordinary acts we practice every day
at home are of more importance to the soul
than their simplicity might suggest."*

–St. Thomas More

Shake out doubt.
Sliced mustard seeds
gather in creases of what you believed,
once. Find them. Remember the feel
of soft, the soap-smell of calm,
and smooth the fabric ridges.

Claim denim and flannel as rosary,
then fold and refold both
like church bulletins.
                              Remember to separate
thick from thin, light
from dark, whole
from holey.
                              Discard completely
the permanently stained, but save
for next week's pre-wash treatment
your favorite ways to wear
the dirt you're drawn to
even on wash day,
even mid-cycle of such
necessary ritual cleansings.
                              Put everything away
in its own neat compartment.
Pray for what you've done—
the diligently muddied, the scrubbed—
and left undone—wine on the sheets,

under-the-bed socks.
Most importantly, rinse and—
even when it resembles chore—

        repeat.

A House Divided

The toppling wakes me
from sleep, that sweet retreat
to denial, the state that makes it
easier to dismiss destruction. Opened eyes
collect dust, allow the beams in
near the iris, adjust the view
dramatically. When pretenses come down,
everything's a window
for catastrophic collapse,
but also Light.
Look, you can see
the sun just to the right
of the wrecking ball.

Mañana

"after this one night I'll cling to her skirts
and follow her to heaven.' With this excellent resolve
for the future, Goodman Brown felt himself justified
in making more haste on his present evil purpose."

−*Young Goodman Brown,*
Nathaniel Hawthorne

"Mañana," we call over our shoulders
to our other selves on the brink of the forest,
the ones testing the shadows with a toe,
calculating the time and temperature of predicted
repentance. "Mañana," we hang on the breeze
drifting toward the dark leaves that decay
beneath our dust-clad feet traveling nowhere
but away. "Mañana, mañana, mañana"—the liturgy
we taste with our dusk-scented tongues, the scarlet-
letter lies we swallow, just as the last lights sink
and—from the thick woods of our denial—
the serpents uncoil.

Adultery

*"One may smile, and smile,
and be a villain."*

–*Hamlet*, William Shakespeare

He lays the lie down and sleeps with it,
a twisted sheet between their turned backs.
On the hard knots of what is not,
he fist-over-fists into her hesitant
submission to sorrow's
coverings, his night lips alternate sips
of remorse, denial. Fabrication
is the tough skin that itches,
peels in unmatched patches.
Soon even bare bones are gone.
A charismatic emperor, he pulls on
his ritual of bright new clothes.

Road Trip

"This illusion trips him. . . . he runs.
Ah: runs. Runs."

                           –*Rabbit, Run,* John Updike

This step-after-step chase to the afterlife
invites detours—dust: the afterthought kicked up
by heels leaving the scene: I run,
you run, he runs, she runs, they run
away, beyond, the body dragging
the last of its soul by a shoelace.

Over deserts, over cliffs,
over lakes—frozen and un—
over hotel Gideons and attic King James,
over *Good News for Modern Man*
and *Book of Common Prayer,*
the feet punctuate their ellipses, pivot
to prodigal or penitent;
you can't tell by the flesh
blistered with persistence.
It's the finish line that knows,
the aching tendons that remember.

Escape

"Nobody ever gets to know no body!
We're all of us sentenced to solitary confinement
inside our own skins, for life!"

–Val in *Orpheus Descending,*
Tennessee Williams

Shuck off the spirit,
un-mind the mind,

fill the flesh so full it flows beyond
ball and socket, bone and skin,

the sermon and sin of isolation.
Or better yet:

Bag the body and its bars,
un-man the mortal with music,

pied-piper the soul
past the confines of term and verdict.

Loner, don't stop to deliberate.
Step beyond the steely skeleton of self.

Take the stringed key
and—sing it—you're free,

Spirit.

Leprosy

I.

Not comfortable in this skin, I scratch
the surface, cover up
the sores of existence, so many
abscesses of absence, pockmarks
of hypocrisy. And then the fingers,
full of loss of touch, start falling off
before limb-for-a-limb and cheek-for-a-cheek
take over. It is all I can do to see
the real with this new
loss of vision.

II.

In the blurred
light between grave and boulder,
St. Damien cleanses the lesions
of the lonely: lepers, those afflicted
with HIV, me. Skin deep
is what he peels
away into sacrifice,
"martyr of charity,"
"leper priest of Molokai,"
moaning only for others
on this self-imposed
island to which I, too, row,
still dry in the safe world
of reading and regret.

III.

Inspiration to Gandhi,
hero to Stevenson,
St. Damien hovers over our homeless
bodies, reminds us to take,
eat, but also to give, living flesh
pressed against the wounds
we quarantine then forget
on some island far
from the continents of respect.

IV.

But also here
where skin has little to wear
outside itself. O epidermis,
such an imperfect fit,
this world putting on
so clumsily new words
on this old skin
of ancient whine.

Memorial Day Weekend

Isla Vista, 2014

On this weekend for honoring the dead,
more dead, the radio blasting updates
between ballads, Beach Boys, the "Battle
Hymn of the Republic."

Friday night post-graduation
in a college town not unlike ours,
sorrow drenched in war songs and the same
bloody questions we've mourned before,
each grief mounting beyond what we feared
possible, now possible again,
the way the radio keeps blaring
Sousa, worst-case scenarios drumming still
worse long after we've tried
to turn the knob, silence the sound waves,
to finally and forever
disconnect the throbbing beat
between each patriotic wave
of the half-mast flag.

July 5th

All the flag-clad *oohs* and *ahhs* fizzle
just past midnight, a slight singe of burn
hovering over today: patriotic hangover
with stars and stripes banging about in brains
that never OK'd reciting names and dates
in 4th grade History. Such a dazzling,
distracting explosion: all that reality behind
the pomp, so ceremoniously like that other
season's parade: winter's green/red (the frigid
red/white/blue) *pa-rum-pa-pum-pummed*
into "Little Drummer Boy" with only tepid recognition
of the day's conviction. Holy Mother
of Jefferson, the fireworks' dizzy outbursts
of *Me! Me! Me!* reveal our belief in nothing
but the day's commemoration, the morning after's
leftover hot dogs or eggnog a hodgepodge of forgotten births:
nation and God piped-in patriotically
as afterthought for the background.

Straw

Rumpelstiltskin could not spin
this into finer fabric.
What held His tiny limbs,
held the world
redeemed,
our sin-stained blood
made royal by His ransom.

It started here
again, the second Adam
pushed out past thighs
toward what feeds
those we keep
locked away
in stables.

From there,
His cries chimed out
beyond the barn
and touched the wise men's
constellations.

Such shimmering straw,
we bless you;
we make of you bright palms!

The JCPenney Advertisement

shouts *4-Hour Doorbusters*
in headliner arrogance
above the full-color page
of bras jutting out
at any middle-aged onlooker
unaware of ironic intent.

My six-year-old daughter asks
explanations for all words:
puns, pundits, sarcasm, snide.
My small son plays drums
on my own sagging breasts.

Meanwhile, we forbid the word *stupid*
in our suburban home,
trying to tame our natural snobbery,
while smiling obnoxiously
at our own bad jokes,
the ones we say on purpose,
with knowledge and intent.

My children love words for their results
and make up jokes disconnected
from any sense. *Why did the refrigerator
go outside? To say hello to the birds.*
It's our joy they wait for,
the laughter we can't keep inside our mouths
that makes them bellow, try another sentence
of nonsense, stringing together syllables
to hook us into their world,

a story so separate from this town,
this state, this continent of innuendos

we read to them straight-faced
from the newspaper, looking for comics
to fold into a metaphor, make fly
all the illiterate letters.

Things

All week, the boxes pile up. The things
my dying mother so fiercely kept
for years, she now fiercely gives to me, all she wants
but can't keep in the small room
she's moving to. "Remember. . . ,"
she says, the same way I tell my teenage son,

"This was how you drew the sun
at four. Why we framed it. One of my favorite things."
He tosses it anyway. "I remember,"
he sighs; "that's enough. It's kept
here," and he points to our cluttered rooms
of heart and brain. A good kid, he wants to pacify, but I want

things and dig it out of his trash. I want
all the scrawled words that were my son
even as our overloaded dining room
collects donations from our lives, a tithing
of each decade: china, postcards, needlepoint chairs kept
a century in storage to remember

great-grandmothers—all my mother's memories
surrounded now by boxes of what my son doesn't want,
which is everything I've carefully kept
to document his life, my lifelong orison
to fend off change reduced to nothing
but nostalgia, recycling, a packed storeroom

of someone else's life. "All our rooms,"
my husband complains, "are other people's memories."
It's true, but some are also mine. And yet, unearthing
old passports from the life I still want,
I let them go into the open bag my son
holds out to help me keep

a life separate from the past, a few seconds that keep
clicking forward instead of back, making room
for other chairs, cards, or crayoned suns
by grandchildren who may or may not remember
to keep what I once kept, to want
my memories along with theirs, the things—

because I love my son—I no longer keep,
the things that in losing give more room
to remember what we have now in this world of want.

A Man in an Armani Business Suit
Waits for the Light

Confidently toting a leather briefcase
a shade lighter than the T-bone I devoured
last week at Maurice's, he stops at *Don't Walk*,
pushes the prescribed button, keeps reciting—
louder than my last ten PowerPoint lectures combined—
apocalyptic revelations, chapter and verse
of horse and rider, bloody plagues, visions, all
while staring straight ahead in his meticulously pressed suit,
past me in my foot-on-the-break new Saab to the other side
of Market. He waits patiently for the right sign
to act, his mouth still moving,
and I look around for some ventriloquist
in jeans and end-of-the-world T-shirt
to continue the damnation/salvation scenario,
but it's just me and the unexpected suit
calmly spouting his proclamations at the 4-way
as he strolls a foot from my front bumper
along the pre-determined path of downtown pedestrians
clustered that moment between man-made lines
just before the light changes and predictable
rush hour traffic continues
the same as yesterday and the day
before that, and the day before that.

The Varsouviana Again

—A Streetcar Named Desire, *Tennessee Williams*

This is how the music goes:

in and out of the *then*, the *now*,
a two-step of death and desire,

the Beautiful Dream of Belle Reve,
the White Woods and the Allan Grey,

simple steps clad in the once-fine
threads of a well-worn waltz

that almost disguises the polka's tones,
common, Polish, and naked beneath the single bulb

undressed now from its Chinese lantern
over the too-hot dance floor

where the orchestra keeps playing—
its only song—gunshot!

This is how the music goes:

swirling and twirling what was,
what ought to have been,

what never happened,
passion and loss partnered imperfectly,

until all that's left to hear
is the beautiful lie

in its grand old house, swaying along
to a radio that keep crackling

how the music goes.

His Memory

"Memory takes a lot of poetic license."

                         –*The Glass Menagerie,* Tennessee Williams

Mixing its cocktail of poverty and pleasure,
it lounges in the heart,
mulls over decades of tête-à-têtes,
and occasionally picks up a pen
with an exaggerated flourish.
Everything it touches is emotion.
It can't be bothered with details
or scene-by-scenes
unless they happened almost
but not quite. If it sounds
good, if it rolls off the tip of the
pencil, if it pours out exactly like
that from the near-empty glass
or the too-full eyes,
then it is,
goddammit, it is.

Initials

Disguised,
you try to hide
the feminine inside
letters; abbreviate the obvious.
(*Katherine* to *K*, *Margaret* to *M*;
Christine and *Patricia* truncated
to editor-accepted ambiguity.)

Girl, what will out
is still woven
between women,
once pumped from the brain
and breast
into the curve
or rigid lure
of words, words
pricked fresh
from the tongue
with the taste
of the forbidden
deliciously
devoured
and handwritten over
to all those waiting
men.

The Woman Up Front

for Virginia Martin, 1930–2012

Inside the young woman's body,
there is a girl learning the world.
Her awkward hips don't quite fit
at the elementary-sized desk
in the crowded college classroom
bordered by hills and a horizon
as wide as what she doesn't know
yet.

She keeps her eyes down,
her lips closed, but she is listening
to something beyond the narrow streets
of her small, pot-holed town.

In the words of the woman up front,
she hears the raspy call of waves,
and she longs to sail, not her own Susquehanna,
but a risky, saltwater trip *To the Lighthouse*
of that other Virginia.

Beneath her cramped desk,
the girl stretches her thin legs.
Her arms, accustomed to balancing
egg-stained plates at the local diner,
move now toward a different memory
where "nothing stays, all changes;
but not words, not paint," and the girl,
in the young woman's body, lifts her hand
an inch, as if writing or painting
a life she just learned existed.

Even now, she knows
that the syllables lining her lungs,
that the half-formed sentences
still afraid to ride the wave of her breath,
that the portraits starting to form in her fingers,
all come from the woman up front
voicing a journey of words the girl yearns to follow.

When the girl looks out
the classroom window,
she begins to see
seascapes curving out
toward a lightly sketched coastline
blessed with a beacon as bright as
the woman up front.

From the water she herself will paint,
she'll craft words, whole boats of hope
floating out to the larger world.

And this girl, now a young woman in a body
that shifts to sit straighter
at a too-small desk in Central Pennsylvania,
opens her mouth to speak
waves of words

while the woman up front
nods and listens
and keeps heading out
To the Lighthouse,
where, together, they'll both turn
and row further into the vast blue
of a future she first heard
from the woman up front.

Fishing for Sestinas

At first, there is only the paper
as plain as sleep without the dream,
as flat as the sea without its waves,
no sound, no ripple, no fish
slipping in and out so
suspiciously. Ah, now write

that, not worrying about wrong or right
but only what floats up to your paper,
what your fishing pole of a pencil tugs so
deliciously toward your eyes. Dream
of letters swish-swishing their fins, of fish
bright as summer minutes, of waves

that twist and flip and cha-cha-cha. Wave
hello and reel them in. Words are your net. Write
a thousand buckets full of fish
that flip about, splash till you and your paper
are soaked with poems and all they dream.
Too many? No need to even sew

up the holes, the poems themselves sew
together our world, the way fish in waves
thread themselves in-and-out, the way dreams
swim their own stories, can write
themselves below the surface, the way paper
can catch even the smallest fish

floating within your mind. Let's fish
together on quiet afternoons so
still you hear the whispers of bluegills. With their paper-
thin scales, they rise above the waves

of your thoughts, trying to write
up their own storm of images. Let's dream

this water together, this lake of dreams
brimming full of rainbow, rhyming fish
that glitter as they leap. Let's write
the entire salty ocean so
full of creatures, they surf the waves,
then scuttle across the flat sand of paper.

Ah, the joy of pencil and paper that dream
such jubilant waves, that fish
for syllables so splendid we cast our lines and write.

To All Those Struggling Women Poets

jostling pen and junior,
computer and comp classes,
lover and love of words—
step in with both feet dripping
with wrung-out dreams;
get your graying hair wet and wet again.
It will not get better. It will
not get easy to feed the few seeds
pushing themselves out
of your dry, crowded,
busy brain, but listen—
when has your life been other
than what's written
here, now?

Gwendolyn,

too cool for the schooled in poetry,
you are again shooting pool at the Golden Shovel,
catching up on Bronzeville gossip with Sadie and Maud.
Of course, the regulars gather quickly,
tipsy enough on your simple elocution.
Your age and kerchiefed grace win you the edge
over others, your eight ball rolling
rhythmically where it should,
iambs waiting patiently in each pocket
for the spinning, clacking, ricocheting
that tilts your small frame,
your large-as-life words,
past the table to all
the wide-eared,
simple folk
who are
who we
are.

Gnarled Branch Outside My Window

that juts up from nowhere and stops
before reaching sky,
misplaced beanstalk not courageous enough
to chance a giant,

my eyes still climb you,
claim the promise of harps,
fresh eggs uncracked and golden.

James and the Giant Peach

From these shadows, spinster aunts
glow with cinematic cruelties,

project full-screen and sharper
than any typefaced fears

devoured decades earlier.
The children hold my hands.

(Last week, I squirmed
at action hero cartoons;

my son explained, "It's okay
when good people shoot bad.")

But here the villains are related,
the parents dead and thus unhelpful,

the Dahl New York fantasy
charismatically written with twin towers

and peach-piercing spires.
We can't eat ourselves out of this one,

though the fruit is luscious
and full of animated bugs.

The story goes on. Between
the popcorn and jujubes,

I have no choice but to endure
all the way to the end.

The Movie

"It is the blight man was born for,
It is Margaret you mourn for."

-"Spring and Fall: To a Young Child,"
Gerard Manley Hopkins

In the dark, we watch a wall
that shimmers light
from a cubicle outside
the almost-empty room.
Somewhere not here, a bird sings,
then plummets toward Goldengrove's
dying. We hear the sad trill in the score,
recognize its ghost of an image
on the decades-old screen,
in its stabbed-in-the-heart theme
cocky enough to stalk the poem
and take its lines hostage.

Even so, the camera has panned
our sorrow perfectly: all the world's
turmoil in that first burst of leaves
dropping their gold as when
Lonergan directs his carefully
orchestrated bus to screech
into distraction, into death,
into all the cinematic close-ups of blame
as weak as Adam's first disclaimer,

as pale as the guilt-stained cheeks of Paquin,
who won't stop screaming incriminations
she can't fix, immortality
thrown under City Transit
thanks to Special Effects
expertly bleeding grief

that even now wells up
in each character and, yes, in us,
Hopkins' autumn as fresh as the credits
flashing their momentary light
as we linger too long
in the familiar local theatre
strewn once again with popcorn
and empty, crushed boxes of Dots.

Winter: Teaching Dante's *Inferno*

March: icy apparitions, frigid prayer,
all good intentions damned to frozen lakes—
or were they good?—the wordcraft of warfare

revises motives, thaws our worst mistakes
to lukewarm doubt, to culture-clutching spin.
And yet the sleet rains down, the once-soft flake

pounds snowy fists, bites suntanned, frost-bound skin.
Hellfire or glacial pit—Christ, sin is sin.

I-80 Proclaimed Safe by Weather.com

Black ice, pretending retreat
on the cold shoulder's road,
camouflages as shadow, schemes,

stretches its shards toward my foot,
which is broken but still breaking
the limit of speed, catapulting

the whole slick week into this
already defeated fortress of a car
as each predestined second skids

into ambulance lights
tottering at the crest of a hill
stacked up with old snow.

There to the left: its globe spins,
shrill blue, splintering. See,
I told you. It's waiting for me.

"Let's Kill All the Lawyers"

—Henry VI, Part 2, 4.2.74, William Shakespeare

Then charge them with inadequate counsel,
bad graveside manners,
unnecessary exploratory excavation
of the worst kind. There must be millions
in each malpractice, in such excess
of "Pain and Suffering" forced down
the ailing physician's throat.
Let's insure premium liability,
a full disclosure of their own
bad-tasting medicine,
cost-free and swift
as Justice unbandaging her eyes
to heal all impatient patients
and vilified victims still waiting
for their overdue appointment
and unforeseen exclusions.

Philosophy

This is a day of this and that tumbling
off the stretched tightrope of time
into whatever isn't going to be—
though the fatalist down the block
who walks in all weather, sleet or shine,
predicts otherwise, cites the sequence of syllables
clicking here. For spite, I delete ten words, start again,
which also is predestined
to drive me mad, prophetically
mapping out the circuitous route
that's already etched centimeters
below the surface. Should I end
here? "Doesn't matter," he sighs.
"Already determined who will read."

Two Thousand Plus

Since childhood we've talked the year
as fantasy, syllables stacked like computer chips,
free-floating sentences orbiting the world
of all we want to happen or fear will be.

What aliens our words are now,
mistranslated in a future
we've already read
and stuck back on the shelf.

Still, time shifts any plot thick
enough to twist with imagination,
reinvent its letters and sounds.

We are forever our own time capsule,
delineated and dated, tenaciously defending
who we thought we could be
when that long-distance future we would be
is just us with another face
looking toward what is still
further beyond.

My Classroom for a Reader

Cowering behind desks,
afraid of everything Elizabethan,
you cringe, terrified of *thees* and *thous*,
the uncounted horror of couplets.

Frailty, thy name is Freshman.
You think too little: such minds are dangerous.
Screw your courage to the sticking place.
Tomorrow, and tomorrow, and tomorrow
is not the time to cram three-hundred pages.

You do protest too much
of dead hard drives and grandmothers.
Hath not a teacher ears, affections, passions?
Cudgel thy brains!

If this were played upon a stage now,
I could condemn it as an improbable fiction:
Macduff, a cop-dog; Ophelia, a drink;
Mercutio, the part that makes an engine whir?
Ah, forsooth and fair speed;
get thee to a dictionary!

Alas, more in sorrow than in anger,
I herein quoth, "'twas caviar to the general";
"the patient must minister to himself."

As brevity is the soul of wit,
you are dismissed!

The English Teacher Contemplates Suicide

but first has to scribe a note
worthy of publication: the stress
of addressing the intelligentsia,
balancing wit and wisdom,
practicing the prose she preaches
paralyzes her. Posthumous

is the way to go, yet
unmixing metaphors is so
mortifying, unconstructing
deconstruction undoable
in a day, much less
those meticulous minutes
it takes to pen
a well performed and poetic

Help! pitiful but pithy enough
for any Plath-loving
parishioner. She breathes
deeply, chooses a pad,
skillfully researches all
inner resources but everything's
checked out. After three

wastebaskets of would-be
winsome epistles, she settles
for near-death, takes up the red pen
once again to mark.

Repeat Checkup

"For there was never yet philosopher
That could endure the toothache patiently. . . ."

−*Much Ado About Nothing,* William Shakespeare

At the root, in the *o* of *howl,*
the un-Novocained pain of excavation,

no patience grows for poetry,
no pithy acceptance of oratory endurance.

The stoics are liars,
their lips trembling

with the same terse curses
and angry anathemas

toward anyone sporting drills
or orthodontia.

Listen to Leonato:
open your mouth and scream.

Pity each of the thirty-two
enameled squares of pain.

Afterwards, you can shoot up
with amnesia or

meditate on your reconstructed memory or
compose insightful epics on

the ontological components
of suffering and the human shriek.

The Other Stroke Patient in the Room with Your Name Said

it was the shooing away,
the incessant irritation,
you, an air traffic controller gone haywire,

pale arms flapping furiously at the stale air
just below her celestial, sequined slippers,
her sweeping ballroom gown, blue as a bedpan,

catching on IVs and monitors
just before she swooped a foot above your brow,
pivoted midair, then circled, circled, circled.

It woke him: your muttering,
the way you caught at her hem,
tried to claw your way to the wings,

kept swatting at the glimmer
of what you weren't
ready for. "The hell with you,"

he said you screamed, "Get out!"
And she did, he told me, swear
to God.

Elegy Ending with Balloons

Little rises in this cold:
half-hearted consolations just so much

steamy breath, this lukewarm earth
not frozen, but stubborn,

unwilling to yield you/us
any rest. Above such dirt,

our fists clench tight to grip
shovels that don't exist.

Instead, from some silly
well-wisher, we hold

balloons, heavy with shriveling
promises of flight,

latex script taunting,
 "Thinking of You."

And yet, suspended midair,
these helium messengers hover

hours, refuse to move
even a coffin's width

from our thick-coated sides.

Again, Death

explodes the day so delicately
we recognize the fissures only
in retrospect: the slight sneer before,
the slanted glance, the beautiful
absence of anything
personal, all intricately stitched
into this portrait of power,
the thin crack tugged,
not lighted, till even our own
threaded logic begins
to unravel.

April 15, 2013

My Son Draws a Picture of the Twin Towers Moments Before a New York Yankees Pitcher Crashes His Plane

October 11, 2006

His caption reads, "This did not happen," but it is happening again
moments after my son points out the flames swirling
from his magic-markered Twin Towers. Beneath one of the windows,
he has written "Help!" in his careful seven-year-old script. "Yes,"
I nod to his eager eyes, but I am trying to answer that cry of anguish
in a month of school shootings and sex scandals. "Help!" I repeat
as I take his drawing to the refrigerator, hold it to the metal surface with
a Guardian Angel magnet I bought yesterday at the new
Anglican bookstore around the corner. What made him draw this now?

When the evening news scrolls across the television set, and he sees
filmed flames—part of his drawing come alive—he gasps,
crosses himself, and runs to the Yankees poster he has taped
to his bedroom door. Who can order tragedy?

Tonight, in his prayers for the dead, he'll begin with family;
move to the Twin Towers, Katrina, and Rita victims; bow his head
for Jackie Robinson and Buck O'Neil; list the Crocodile Hunter
and Maynard Ferguson; the slain Amish girl; the high school students.
Maybe he'll stumble over the last names, look up, and ask for help. Help.

Seek and Ye. . . .

"Where there is no love,
put love—and you will find love."

                        –St. John of the Cross

But where it is—this promise of
reap-after-sow, get-after-give, find-after-look,
cheek-after-turn, rise-after-down, live-after-
-not-happily—where it is
slipped in or slashed open
or stomped on or   Where it is?
Elusive as air, as omniscience, as prayer
trip-tripping these clay feet
indefinitely; one glance of your askance
gaze, and the *un* comes clattering off
conditional just when I begin
hope-against-hope to believe
I can see.

Confession

Same lazy list of nothing

bold.	No sins
killed:	impatience,
lies, anger	still
kicking, still	karate-
chopping	seconds,
milliseconds	even;
unflashy, bland sins	defiant, standing
up to leave	but never leaving
entirely,	stomach-punched
by the priest,	then blood-flushed
from God's	eye but still
in mine,	those splintered
irritants,	such strong
tiny	crosses

right in the retina.

Rocking Chair Hymn

And praise be this chair
with its waltz of the heart
that dips with the breeze
and the lilt of the lark.
And praise the pulse there
in the stretch of the limbs
in both person and tree
as we two-step with Him
in the motion of nature,
the beat we breathe in,
the rhythm of earth,
the dance and the hymn.

Mission to Play

*"Jabari Parker Heeds NBA's Call,
Bypassing Formal Mormon Mission"*

      —*New York Times* headline, 6/25/14

Six feet, eight inches of *Sweet Jesus*
dribbled into your home in living color,
a *hallelujah* of slam dunks and triple-doubles,
three-point plays proselytizing as much as any
white-shirt-wearing, door-knocking man on a mandated mission
to get you off your inherited holey couch and onto a pew
chiseled from his great-grandfather's conversion
a hundred years ago in Tonga. It's a live ball, so listen
to the hymn of whistling referees,
their black-and-white thinking almost ready
to pivot into eternity. The game clock keeps ticking,
and ESPN cameras zoom in
waiting for the NBA's MVP play
of faith to jump-start
a new, rowdy crowd
ready to crash
the boards.

Repeat Occurrence

Unaware of the unexpected
always crashing toward us,
my niece sleeps faithfully into her teens
beneath a canvas tent. Soon, her best friend's skull
will crack beneath a collapsing oak.
My niece will turn in her sleeping bag to see
what could have been her blood,
and then she'll forget, the pain
too vivid to hold in any synapse.

Even so, this is a story of two
survivals and one boy she doesn't know,
dead on the stretcher, his shocked father
looking on, unable to save

the way I want to save her
and her young friend
from what creaks and topples in this world,
threatening to uproot even our deepest
fibers tunneling through
yet more unexplained
territories of terror.

Yet Another

11/13/15, 12/2/15

Was sky ever other than this:
smear of ocean hovering over
Noah's thick-tarred ark,
omen of gray replaying
more-of-the-same torrents?

All soaked memories rise with this wet
horror of loss, wash our muddied hope
out to the sea we now believe in
daily. Where is that small boat of faith?
Where the drowned Icthus
willing to swim above
the coming waves?

Esau's Lament

Without your words   my breath cracks
     dust on sand   without your words
my limbs break   bones on graves
Oh my father   me too   without
     Can even this be stolen?   your words
No syllables of blessing left?
      No mouthed morsel of hope?   Oh my father
I alone am the hunted   your words
     trapped and slain   me too
the spoils stolen again   me too
      that fair enemy
               without without

Transposition

"Dazed with fear, Okonkwo
drew his machete and cut him down.
He was afraid of being thought weak."

–*Things Fall Apart*, Chinua Achebe

There—machete
raised high to the heavens—
his perfect fear cast out love,
Ikemefuno's sudden cry the opposite of Isaac's.
No angel swooping in. No ram bleating in the bush.
No shouts foreshadowing New Testament paraphrases
of 1 John 4:18. Just the stranglehold of fear. Just
his surrogate son's "Father, they have killed me!"
interrupting the long journey home.

Jacob Wrestles with God

—Genesis 32:22–32

What daring, and only a wrenched hip
and changed name to stumble home on.

Israel, we call you now,
    you who pinned God and forced a blessing,

    who pressed Yahweh's face to the ground and lived.
O Deceiver, who stole your brother's birthright.

O Defrauder, who duped a blind father;
    faithful fighter, strong-holding the Strong,

    how mightily the Almighty must love you,
His mercy overpowering

the flimsy might of your muscles,
    the bruised strength of your repentant soul.

"If He Who Can Does Not, It Must Be Better So,"

the deacon with a doctorate preaches his punch line
decades after the woman with cancer pleads
to be saved but isn't, though her family is.

With his doctorate and his punch line,
the deacon preaches cancer and the woman who is
not—though her family is

clinging to the cross at her grave,
howling their repentance—the woman
also is. Decades later, the deacon preaches

how the doctor cannot save, how cancer
punches pain until repentance
pleads its saving line of what is

decades later. After the woman
preaches her life of cancer, we cling
to the deacon's lines. To be saved

is and isn't a howling decade's worth
of cancer. Waiting for repentance,
we cling to our doctorates. The cross

pleads from cancer's grave, "It must be
better so," and our pain lines up
to howl. The deacon with his pain

preaches the cross, and we plead
to be saved—though our family doesn't.
"It must be better so" preaches

a pain that howls decades. To be saved
is the line we cling to when His grave empties.
The deacon with the cancer preaches pain

and graves. We cling to his lines
like repentance and save what isn't.
And it is better so.

Bookmark

First, do no harm. Steer your mouth's words and heart's meditations
clear of fear and judgment. Uncurl your tongue with love and language.
Savor the story. Look up. Practice stepping away from the page.
Let the lines and Spirit speak for themselves without
sounding brass or tinkling cymbals.

Belief and Blackboards

The writing on the state
school's slate, the wall, or the stone
of ten clear non-cursive commandments
all clutter different dimensions
here.

Still,
sometimes I see
a film of lamb's blood across the lintel
or flakes of manna in the unexpected snap
of chalk, the blank stare of a stalled
video, the discarded syllabus
crumpled and tossed on the tile. Or

when the skies slash and thrash with rain,
and the room pools with shadows, I see
stigmata, small but perfect in the unexpected
hand raised charismatically in the last row.

I see so many ascensions: eyes hearing.

Across the hall, my colleague tosses
"stupid," "blind," "insipid" at her class,
teaches them to laugh at everything
crisscrossed with worship. Beneath
florescent lights, she howls
at the joke of holiness.

And then a sparrow pecks at the window:
wanting us, wanting in.
His beak chips at our thoughts,
an awkward metronome.

My class and I turn back
to Herbert and metaphysics;
in retaliation, discard our chalk or pens.

A student I thought asleep
starts to read,
his thrush of a voice
syncopated by the bird's insistence.

And this is all we need:
the real, the spiritual, the Real;
the thin laughter in the background;
the crescendo of the poem rising, covering each desk,
each tile: floor and ceiling.

Acknowledgments

The author gratefully acknowledges the following publications where poems first appeared, sometimes in earlier versions.

"Again, Death," *Relief*

"Adultery," *Hawaii Pacific Review*

"Belief and Blackboards" (in an earlier version), *Windhover: A Journal of Christian Literature*

"Confession," *Seminary Ridge Review*

"Esau's Lament" (in an earlier version), *Christian Century*

"Escape," *The Southern Quarterly: A Journal of Arts & Letters in the South*

"Euchre and Eucharist," *Seminary Ridge Review*

"Father's Day," *It's About Time* (Main Street Rag)

"Fishing for Sestinas" (under another title), *String Poet*

"The Fourth Man," *Dappled Things*

"Gwendolyn," (in an earlier version), *The Same*

"How Spiritual Are You?" *Ascent*

"A House Divided," *The Other Journal*

"If He Who Can Does Not, It Must Be Better So," *St. Katherine's Review*

"Initials," *Women's Studies*

"Invention," *My Cruel Invention* (Meerkat Press)

"The JCPenney Advertisement," *Relief*

"The Joke Around the Water Cooler and Other Dilemmas," *First Things*

"July 5th," *New Verse News*

"Laundry List," *First Things*

"Leprosy," *Adanna*

"Louise" (under a different title), *Women's Studies*

"Lower, Higher Ed," *First Things*

"Memorial Day Weekend," *New Verse News*

"Mission to Play," *Curator*

Acknowledgments

"My Son Draws a Picture of the Twin Towers Moments Before a New York Yankees Pitcher Crashes His Plane," *Relief*

"No Shadow of Turning," *Anglican Theological Review*

"On Defining Education," *Every Day Poems*

"The Other Stroke Patient in the Room with Your Name Said" *Relief*

"Parable," *First Things*

"Philosophy," *The Same*

"Prayer" (in an earlier version), *Anglican Theological Review*

"The Prophecy of Birds" (in an earlier version), *Christian Century*

"Repeat Checkup," *The Cresset*

"Road Trip," *Christian Century*

"Swept Away," *Windhover: A Journal of Christian Literature*

"Teaching Frost," *Watershed: The Journal of the Susquehanna*

"To All Those Struggling Women Poets," *Women's Studies*

"The Varsouviana Again," *Valley Voices: A Literary Review* (Best of the Past Ten Years Issue)

"Two Thousand Plus," *It's About Time* (Main Street Rag)

"Yet Another," *Anglican Theological Review*

"Watch vs. Warning," *New Verse News*

"Winter: Teaching Dante's *Inferno*," *Anglican Theological Review*

Additional thanks to my mother, Roberta Scurlock, from whom I inherited a love of reading; to poets Sofia Starnes, Barbara Crooker, and Julie Moore, for conversations on faith, literature, and life; to D. S. Martin, for his strong insights; and especially to Gary R. Hafer, for his good eye and good heart.

COLLECTIONS IN THIS SERIES INCLUDE: